ROUNDUP

Other poetry titles published by author:

A Country Mile
City Journey
Net Worth

ROUNDUP

Ruth G. Reichbart

VANTAGE PRESS
New York

Cover design by Susan Thomas

FIRST EDITION

Published by Vantage Press, Inc.
419 Park Ave. South, New York, NY 10016

Manufactured in the United States of America
ISBN: 0-533-15447-2

Library of Congress Catalog Card No.: 2006900256

0 9 8 7 6 5 4 3 2 1

Contents

ROUNDUP

Prediction

I dance with ghosts
Most every night
The music is all in my head.
I dance with ghosts
Quite out of sight
'Cause all my loves are dead.

They dance with music
Now fast, now slow.
My eyes are shut, as I said
It matters not
How my feet go,
'Cause all my partners are dead.

But I still hear
All of the tunes
We used to know so well
I dance with ghosts I don't know where
In Heaven or in Hell?

I'll join the ghosts
Sometime I know
It may be hard to tell
As long as we dance
We shall outlast
Heaven, and outlast Hell.

Finale I

Unable to move mountains,
And utterly unsuited to a tightrope,
With no aptitude for the mundane,
I shall henceforth devote myself
To the easiest:
The new book of poems,
The f m symphony
So simple to turn off,
The chance acquaintance
Never allowed to become a friend.

From now on, fellows,
You can find the depths.
I shall carefully
Cling to the surface.

Safe Harbor

Becalmed, I hear the hurricane.
It whips the waves to foam.
It beats the shore with bulging tides,
But I am safe at home.

Becalmed, I see the lightning strike.
It whips through purpled air.
It sears across the clouded night.
I sit and comb my hair.

Becalmed, I taste the salt sea spray.
It leaps into the night.
It screams through wind "Awake! Awake!"
I smile, and shun the fight.

Becalmed, I watch the flying birds
Askitter through the sky,
Their frantic wings are only theirs
No stormbeat bird am I.

Becalmed, I stretch and yawn again,
And shrug, and close my eyes,
No more the storms can call me hence.
I laugh at angry skies.

—1964

Across the Way

Life is but a little story
As the figures come and go.
All the faces that I saw there
Gone forever, moving slow.
I can see them all before me
See the neighbors 'cross the way,
Tall and slender in the garden
Gardening hat and gloves so neat,
I can see the gravel pathway
To the side veranda lead,
And can smell the sweet narcissus
Hear the hum of bees that feed
On the honey of the lilac,
On the apple blossoms feed.

Sunlight of the Adirondacks
Wove its wonder through the air.
I can see a neighbor whittle
With a jackknife, toys so rare.

All are gone, with golden shavings
Into splintered winter air.
Gone and gone are all the neighbors
Those who sang and gardened where
Summer sunlight on the gravel
Painted full my childhood there.

No Return

There's no one I know on the street
Though people are slamming doors,
Cars still standing in driveways,
Wild strawberries growing in ditches,
All have been killed by the salt.

Ten-ton trucks travel in safety
Where horses pulled sledges.
The cows and the chickens have vanished
The children who played in the leaf heaps
Are gone from the sidewalks and woodpaths.

To go back is to see ghosts emerging,
Familiar names only on gravestones,
And the days going by.

Life Sentence

A badly writ story
Without any moral
All background and noise
All mimed without poise
Unbalanced and slow
With nowhere to go,
A prison of days,
Barred in by bleak nights,
With one way out only,
And no help in sight.

—1979

Neighbors

Their references are not mine,
Their heavens not my own
My stars are not under their sign
I go my way alone.

Their childhood days were bleak and sere,
Black rocks above the tide
While mine led down to valley floor
Where summer never died.

So, when we meet we nod, and pass
As distant as a star
That slants its way across the sky
And glistens from afar.

2002

It's too late now.
The town is dead,
The pines, the maples overhead
Have died, and long ago the elms
Crashed down.
Macadam has obscured the ways
Where flowers grew in better days,
Wild strawberries as sweet as sin,
No longer flourish. Now, begin,
Recount the losses would take long.

The beauty that began this song
Has vanished with the century
There is naught left for anyone
For the old village is gone and done.

The Planetarium

The galaxies are nothing but child's play.
The planets toys for children to enjoy.
The explanations are so simple. They
Can be divined by any girl or boy.

But I prefer the brilliant autumn skies,
Outdoors at night. There's no one to explain
The reason why the sullen autumn wind
Should bring both shifting joy and lasting pain.

Yes, keep your explanations to yourself.
For only mysteries are real to me.
Your feeble stuttering puts out the stars.
And brings a darkness I need never see.

Let all the clouds that pass across the sky
Be water mist or wandering galaxy.
I care not so I look at them, and breathe
The icy crispness of the autumn sea.

Fair Warning

Don't you tell me what to do
For I'll take no gup from you
Don't you ever tell me what to do.

If you want to keep me close
You had best not be verbose,
And just never tell me what to do.

The City

At night the traffic growls alone
Like a starved beast
With a bare bone.
At night the lonely sea makes moan,
And beats upon the sullen sand.
At night I wake and hear their cry

While others sleep and only I
Record unwillingly, with fear
Sounds made for some immortal ear,
And not for mine.

Reminiscence I

The heart is a fool.
No matter how often the head
Says "Don't"
The heart will jump
At a look, at a voice, and a lump
Will rise in the throat
At a scene long since mist,
At a lake that is sunk into mud,
An auto that's turned into rust.
I have saved from the world
What like, and the rest
Can go to the deuce,
For the world is an ass.
And there's no one I care
To impress.

—1966

Compensation

As you grow older
The blood slows to colder,
The skin, especially, thickens.
One no longer sickens
At sneers, at looks,
And no longer takes credence
At what one finds in books,
No longer cares
for stares,
And there is something risible
In becoming
Invisible.

—1966

Vale

My ambitions have burst
Like a bowlful of bubbles,
And now I can tell
They were my worst troubles.

Statement

That was a thousand years ago
When all the world was white as snow,
Was green as grass, was bright as rain,
I shall not see that world again.

Now all the world is blind with drink,
And deaf with sound, and out of touch,
And when this world turns itself off,
I shall not miss it much.

Surrounded

One should talk only with strangers,
Holding them at a distance.
Make certain they don't become friends,
Then there is the bare possibility
That you may possess your own soul.

—1965

The Survivor

Today, new tragedies do not exist
They are too late.
Nothing can harm the dead,
All yester scenes have faded.
Like ancient photographs crumbling to dust
When each new day is always grey and white.
There is no color in the sky or tree.
All sounds grow dull and dim and far away
And sidewalks made of cardboard fade to clay.

Mankind in the 20th Century

You poisoned the rivers,
Your grandsons are drug fiends
Polluted the skies,
And your daughters are whores.
You have torn down your cities
To wallow in garbage
You have buried your children
Before they were born.

You have cut down the forests,
And turned plains to desert
Your sins are too many
To list in a year.

You have brought deep destruction
To oceans and meadows,
Extinct are the fish
And the fowl of the air.

And when you have followed
Them all to extinction,
The rats and the roaches
May still well be there.

When your last delirium
Will free Earth forever
And the horrid mistake
That was made in creating you
May then be forgotten

May then be forgiven,
A bad dream once over,
A bad dream that never was there.

Advertisement

Lost. In a melange of dirty dishes
In carpets to be swept
And old clothes washed,
One life.
Return it to

—A. Ghost

Winter in Etown, Indoors

The deerhead
Above the cedar mantel
Stared.
The cobblestones
Of the fireplaced wall
Gleamed.
Outdoors night roared

But indoors
A bit of the sun
Was caught among the cobbles
Glinting from the deerhorns
To the fire
Murmuring
Of past autumnal afternoons
As a twig cracked
Somewhere, underfoot.

Eclogues

I went to see my poor old Pa
A time or two ago,
And he was languishing in town
Amid the ice and snow.

I asked him why he'd not gone South.
The sun was winter warm.
He said there was no place for him
Without a winter storm.

I said he'd lost the farm because
He would not give it up.
He should have sold when things were good,
Not sold it to a pup,

Who owned a bank, and owned some farms,
And wanted all he saw,
But no, he shook his head and said
(I might have known my Pa).

He said that taxes were too high,
He would not make a deal.
He'd rather let it all be lost
Than sell a single field,

Where he had walked since he was small,
Where he had plowed and reaped,
Where he had seen the harvest high,
So full and golden heaped.

Where he had seen the sky in storm,
And seen the sky in sun.
For him to sell the sky in age,
No, he was not the one.

He still could drive to his old fields,
And count the icy stars,
By watching them he'd keep a bit
Of the world that once was ours.
My poor old Pa still lives in town,
A-dreaming of the past.
The family farm is dead and gone.
For nothing good will last.

A Century of War and Revolution

Between one breath and the next
There is silence, for the deaf.
Between one war and the next
There is the click of bayonets preparing.

At night factories roar
Piling bombs.
While body bags are sorted into rows
Waiting for the next round.

All over the planet
Women struggle in childbirth
Bringing infants into a world
Made for killing.

We, swift footed amid the jungle
Sidestep bullets
Till we find death, an anticlimax,
To our wars.

—1988

Catalogues

From flowers to fashion,
Ceramics to cake
They beg you to read them,
To buy or to bake.

From music to mishna.
Cucumbers to palms
They seek your attention
With colors and psalms.

You can dance to the music.
You can paint every day.
You can cook till you're dizzy,
You can drink till you sway.

There's not one that tells you.
There's not one to say
"Just sit and be quiet,
And savor today."

—1988

Query

Dark the clouds,
Deep the rain,
Bitter the dust they carry
Dark the thoughts
Deep the pain.
What fool would go marry?

—1966

Inevitable

It must be radar.
When I try to learn a new piece
On the piano.
The telephone rings.

Sometimes I haven't even started.
Sometimes I finish the first theme.
Sometimes I complete a prelude.

But, should I want the phone to ring.
I sit down at the piano.

—1988

*　　*　　*

The list grows longer every day
The list of those who used to say
"Good morning," in a cheerful way
To me, a cheerful child.

The winds whose voices used to say
"Look up, the sky is here to stay
While downward grows the narrow way,
For me, the vanished child."

His voice repeats,
"The old grey mare
Ain't what she used to be, ain't what she used to be,"
And, "People live too long today,"
"Hello, Sweetheart," this I know, and
"They got the gimmees, greedy things."

All gone the voices once so clear,
Forever silent, save to me,
The faces I shall never see
The days that were can never be.

Sic Transit

Light up the room
Here grows
A chair, blue,
A couch, black,
Music stand,
Books, in case
Curtain, lace
Here
This moment, this year.

Finale II

Too many griefs
Dry up the throat,
Close up the lips,
And turn the eyes
To stone.
Too many griefs
Dry up the blood
And turn the flesh
To bone.
Too many griefs
Tell me
I lie alone.

Garden Note

Oh, the weeds and the ivy that poisons grow free,

But the seeds that I plant are quiescent, like me.

Notes of a Traveller

Just got back from a journey to Hell.
Rounded up some data at the last hotel.
Its walls are papered with comic strips.
And the adventures of hot lips,
The dining room's done in yellow and red.
For a special rate, you get orange instead.
And the waiters enjoy dropping things on your head.

The bellboys all drop things on your toes.
As they cheerfully say that the windows won't close.
Of course, it's quite warm.

There are things former guests have left in the rooms,
Unemptied ashtrays, toothbrushes, whiskbrooms
Seem to swarm.

There's a nonturnoffable radio
And a TV musical comedy show
You listen whether you will or no.

All the light chairs are nailed to the floor.
The handle is gone from the closet door.
There's not a good smell.

I didn't stay long, not very long, well
It's costly these days to live well in Hell.

Remembrance

Somewhere on the other side of tomorrow
Clean water flows over sand and stones
Down the narrow brook where children wade
Seeking to build a dam.

The water, escaping,
Runs over rocks in the shallow tan river
Where sunlight skips, dazzling
Up to the old stone steps.

Once, long-skirted ladies
Stepped from old rowboats
To picnic grounds near the river,
Wearing huge hats, and smiling.

Now only leaves float on the river.

The children huddle back to the woods.
The years snicker by, with the children
And the dream has gone.

Decline

Still standing, like a hollow tree
That stubborn clings unto its rock,
And bows not to the icy blasts,
Awaiting nothing but decay.

Perhaps one branch is still in leaf
When summer's merry breezes blow
Where once the myriad shading leaves
Brought sweets and hush into the air.

The most its ages creaking says,
Serves to proclaim what once was there.
It looks its best in winter air.

Long Ago

The yellow lamplight stains the silent room.
No footsteps now. The doorbell,
Rusts.
The telephone no longer clangs its voice.
The night, left to itself dreams on and on.
A wooden swing reflects the voices of
Six singing children through the summer air.
Sang evening into night.
The lamplight gleamed
Through maple leaves onto the listening grass.
A breath of summer, and a tiny cloud.
The light is gone. The wooden swing is dust.
The maple trees are shattered, and their leaves.

No longer haunt the grass.
The voices still
Ring to my ears
As sweet as nightingale
Throughout the icy, ancient winter night.
Throughout the icy, longtime, storied night.

Summary

Civilization
Is rusting tin cans,
Slender, bright aircraft
And scizofreud mans.

Anticlimax

By the time the bomb hits us
In a day or a year,
We shall be past horror,
We shall be past fear.

By the time the blaze chars us
In a month or a week
We shall be past grieving
We shall no more speak.

By the time the blast slays us
Be we slave or ghost,
We shall be past this day
When we lost the most.

Madrigal

The lad he went a-wooing
And ended up by stewing
Because the gal he's after
Did just dissolve in laughter.
He stalked away in fury,
And said that any jury
Would find him faultless should he
strangle that gal, but could he?
And as he turned away,
She said, "You've made my day."

Doll House

They made it all of cardboard.
The windows had no glass.
The paper dolls looked out with glee
To see the people pass.

The roof was painted lilac
The door was painted green.
The steps were made of pebbles,
The prettiest ever seen.

The owners were two children,
One blonde and one dark-haired,
I saw them eighty years ago,
I wonder how they fared.

Prediction

And when my ashes
Tossed upon the sea,
Storm-tossed Atlantic,
Where they may arrive
At other lands
Where I have never been,
My restless spirit
Contented for a space,
May really rest awhile.

Today

A desert range
Trails off into the sky,
Sandy and dull
With shadows purple, trailing.
There is no road, for
Emptiness abounds.
Even the sands are still,
No wind can move the air.
That, leaden, shields the empty days from view.

There is no path.
No footsteps mar the sands,
And no bird flies
Over the sullen, empty lands.

Reminiscence II

Oh, we were beautiful back there in the thirties.
We were naïve, we thought we could make things better,
But no one would listen.

Now things have changed, the whole world is different,
A whirlwind of gadgets, and prisons.
Now, not only men sleep in shelters,

The children are homeless, over a million today
No one will shelter the children.
No one feed them in prisons.

Our politicians
Vomit their lies on the tube.
An era of unequaled prosperity,
That's what they call it.

America, a word learned in high school
There must have been a place like it
Somewhere, where I never was.

Singing

Let us sing the old songs
The old songs, the old songs.
Let us sing the old songs
We all used to know.

Let us sing the old songs,
The sweet songs, the sad songs.
Let us sing the old songs
We sang long ago.

Through the perfumed summer evenings
We would sit and sing those songs.
Through the moonlit summer evenings
Our clear voices would ring out.
We were young and strong and poignant
In the Adirondack air
Now our voices cracked and anxious
Make believe we still are there.
Let us sing the old songs
The great songs, the sweet songs
Let us sing the old songs
In the freezing air.

Credo

When I'm behaving very well
I know I'm on the road to Hell.
The only times that I find good
Are when I don't act as I should.

Office Parties

Oh for the sunny, bygone days
Before I heard of office parties.
Before I listened to the jokes
So often spoke by office smarties.
When Christmas still meant Santa Claus
Instead of booze in cups of cardboard
And paper plates, and plastic spoons
Bland dips all leaning off to starboard.

Oh for the lovely afternoon
Undimmed by countless Seasons Greetings
And offices bores with outstretched hands,
And office's unwanted meetings.
But if I fled to outer space
I'm sure I'd find the same routinings
Awash with Xmas cards
And all the similar old gleanings.

In the City

I spend my days in the city
Where houses and byways are crowded,
There is no time to be silent,
Leaves are all glued to the trees.

Hearses leave daily, on schedule
Taking their burdens out somewhere.
None will remember their absence.

Someone repaints the apartment,
Someone slips into the carspace.
The seat on the train is not empty.
No one will notice at all.
In the sea of anonymous faces
Someone has drifted away.

My Life

A movie I was in
That cannot be replayed,
The film is lost.
The players scattered
No longer posture
In their faded robes.
No one remembers
When the colors went,
How measured were the songs,
How danced the leaves
Upon the trees now harvested or dead,
And the production
Finished and forgot.

Prayer for the Jewish Dead

Cover the mirrors and draw the blinds,
And sit without shoes on the floor,
Say what you will, the dead won't mind.
They have gone onward before.

No more to suffer, and no more to strive,
They have left all that behind.
Whisper the kaddish, or shout with a roar.
The past is a face that is blind.

"The past is a bucket of ashes."
Where peace is nowhere to find.
Cover the mirrors, and whisper your prayers,
The dead have forgotten whatever was rotten.
The dead have left you behind.

—2000

Vista

We were children, laughing children
Running fast through rain and snow,
As we ran and laughed together
Running fast as we could go.

Now we tread a slower measure,
Those of us who still are here,
We must carefully go onward,
Most of us are underground.

And to look at us, you wonder
If we ever laughed and played.
Are we making up these stories?
Listen how these stories sound.

We were children, singing children.
And our eyes were bright and clear.
We could run as fast as lightning,
But that was another year.

Encounter

Today I saw a bluejay
On the ailanthus tree.
He stayed only a moment,
And never looked at me.

I stood behind the window,
And watched him fly away,
But now the day is brighter.
The sky is not so grey.

Destiny

In another world where I used to be
Three thousand years ago
I used to dance, I was the dance,
A snowflake in the snow,
In that other world where the desert swims
Forever the sun will hover.
Among the sands in that other world
My spirit waits
For this life to be over.

—1966

New Year's Eve

It's midnight in Manhattan,
But here, it's only ten,
And now in Colorado
We shall begin again.

Time travel takes us backward
To times that once we knew,
When we were young and hopeful
To see the future through.

The future has escaped us.
It has become the past.
And we know that time travel
Is nothing that will last.

It's midnight in Manhattan
The New Year's come in view,
While here we're stuck in yesterday
And hope we'll see it though.

To the Young

Hold fast your dreams:
One glimpse of truth
Is all one gets,
And that is youth.

The rest are lies.
Through all the years.
Hold fast your dreams,
Hold fast your tears.

Good-bye Song

When you come to the end,
And it's history
The love that had seemed so strong
Wasted away to a gossamer ghost
There is nothing left but a song.
And the song that looks
From a lost love's eyes
Is stronger than steel,
And tells lovely lies
So that I can say
With a smile on my face
There once was a heaven
Or some such place
A love that lived for a little while,
That is gone, that is gone, that is gone.